MOUTHING OFF

MOUTHING OFF

on the flip of a century

La NoNika

Edited by Joanne Worsley

Fighting Talk

For the ravers and the festival heads, the long weekends 'out' out, the moody Tuesdays and the summers of love. I'm not sure what happened to the Nineties, I lost my grip somewhere in the late Eighties. I wrote a lot of poetry, raved my tits off and clung ineffectively to my sanity, I also had babies and got an education but I'm not sure how I managed that. I didn't really get a proper grasp on it again till way into the Noughties. Now that I have made it to the Twenties, relatively unscathed, I'd like to share some the fruits of the lost years with all and sundry.

With measured gratitude to Pirate Princess, for 'getting' me without further explanation, knowing what the right questions are, perceiving the order of things and for gifting me her precious time and considerable skills in constructing this collection. Your communication style has fortified my self reliance.

Reluctant, but genuine, acknowledgement to Precious, for providing me with challenging spaces to develop and perform the works herein. The resilience I developed is a strength that I would not be without.

And, above and beyond the rest of us, for the boys, who were trying to have a childhood whilst we, their parents, were trying to work out who we were and how to adult in the late 20th Century. I applaud your tenacity, your genius and your diversity, at least you're all good looking and talented. I apologise for the myriad failures, I hope some of it was fun. It was our best.

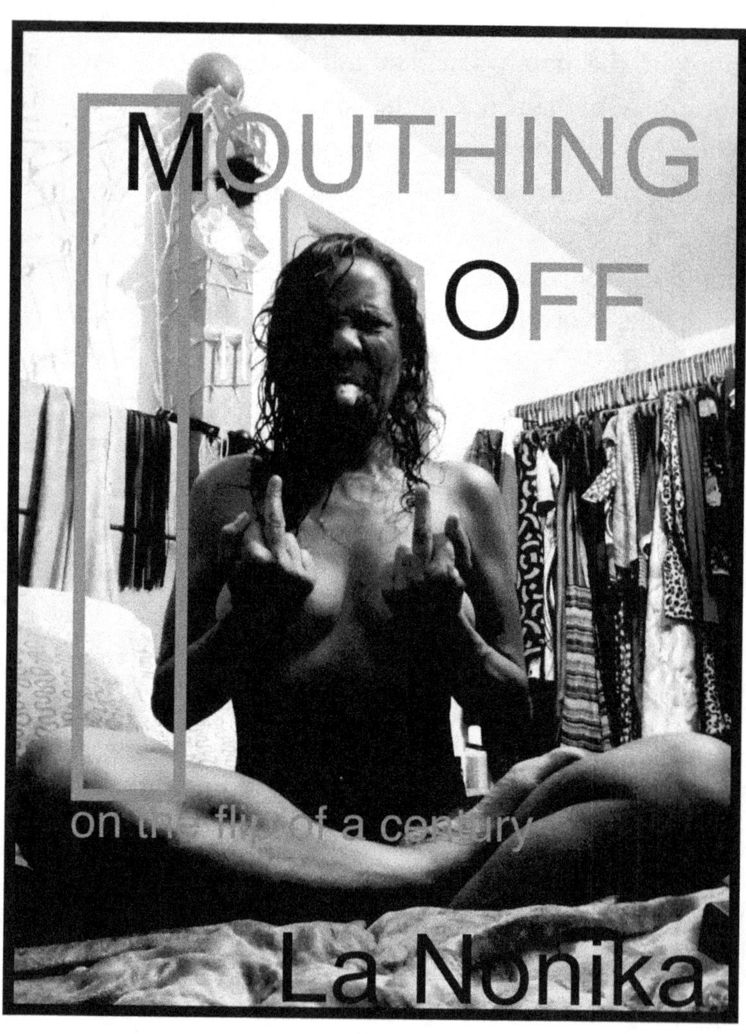

Cover Girl
La Nonika

OVER . Munting

. As You Like It

. On my own head

. Blinding

. Cunt

MY . Safe as Houses

. Faithless

. Born to Shop

. Working for The Mouse

. Without a paddle

. Mine

. Slices of Life

. To Market, To Market

. To Those Of Us Who Would Bear Arms

. Pester Power

DEAD . Shut the Fuck Up!

. Really? Is this how it is?

. Yearn, part one, At A Loss?

. Yearn, part Two, Is It Hometime?

BODY . N.O.C

. I'll hum it, You Play It

. The Hand that Rocks the Cradle

. Kitchen Songs

. Out of the Dolls House

. In Our Time

. Restart

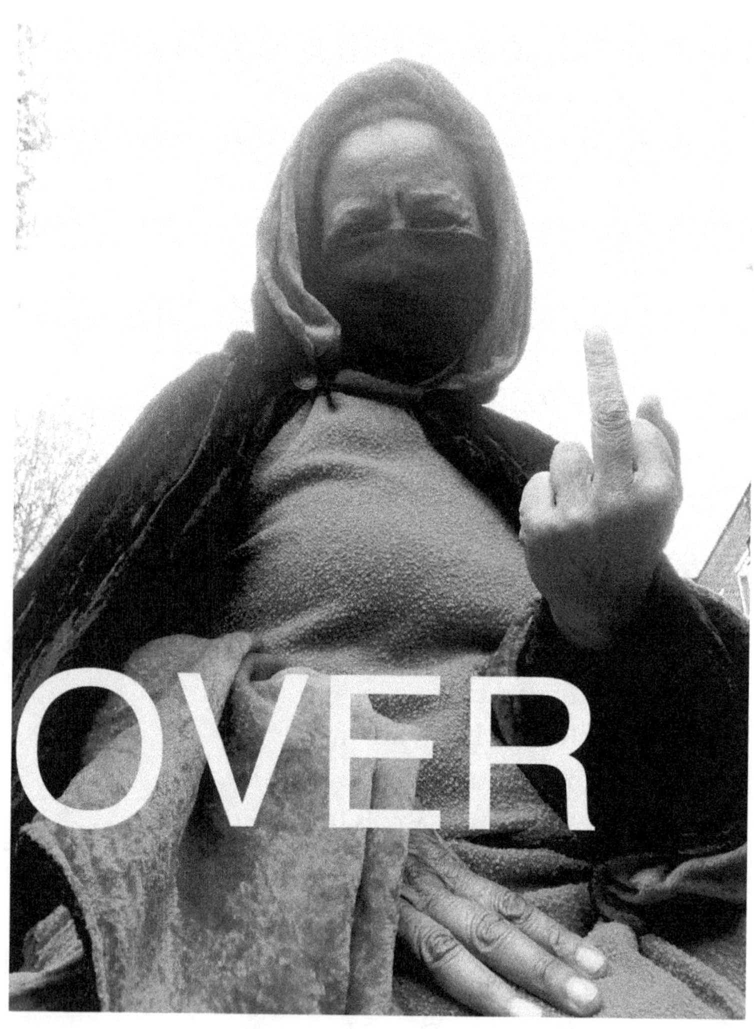

OVER my dead body
La Nonika

Munting

Do I want the blue pill or shall I take the red?
Do I have to choose or can I have them both instead?
Which one makes me larger ?
Which one makes me small?
Which one shows me eternity?
Can I have them all?
Take me to the candy man
He gives me sweets to eat
Take me down the rabbit hole
I'm liking what I see
Did I meet you on the dance floor?
Did I see you in the rave?
Did I feel your skin against me?
Did I lick your pretty face?
Did I feel you move against me?
Did we melt into those tunes?
Did we grind into the music?
Did we rub up in that groove?
Will you come and sweat with me
Rant and rave, get wet with me
Will you come, turn me on
Keep me rushing through till dawn
Let the DJ set you free
Drown you in his fantasy
Let the rhythm move right through you
Let the ecstasy abuse you
I like to feel the pumping bass
So deep inside my belly
Like the way it turns my head

Turns my sweating limbs to jelly
I like reaching for the lasers
I like roaring with the crowd
I like to feel the floor vibrating
Like to hear the music loud
Do I want the blue pill or shall I take the red?
Do I have to choose or can I have them both instead?
Which one makes me larger, which one makes me small?
Which one shows me eternity?
Can I have them all?
As high as a kite
As free as a bird
Like nobody's watching
And I've never been hurt
Like I don't need the money
Like I never felt shame
Like I wanted to film it,
The love that I made
Like there is no tomorrow
Like it grows on trees
Like it lasts forever
Like you get it for free
Take me to the candy man
He gives me sweets to eat
Take me down the rabbit hole
I'm liking what I see
It rocks
It heaves it booms it pumps
It twists and writhes
It screams and jumps

It's a fever
It's a flame
And we will never be the same
It's a buzz
It's a bet
Our communion in sweat
Do I want the blue pill or shall I take the red?
Do I have to choose or can I have them both instead?
Which one makes me larger, which one makes me small?
Which one shows me eternity?
Can I have them all?
My hands in the air and the sweat in my eyes
I spin and I turn and I dance and I rise
The bass in my belly the tunes in my ears
The sweat on my skin and the bodies so near
The sway of the crowd
The lure of the beat
The moment the madness
So fleeting so sweet
It drips from the system and onto my lips
The taste of the rave is a smile, is a kiss
Is a bitter concoction I put on my tongue
Is a bottle of water, is snogging someone
Take me to the candy man
He gives me sweets to eat
Take me down the rabbit hole
I'm liking what I see

As you like it
Rough and ready wins the race
In your mind and on your face
On your lips and in that place
Go there, do it, flout disgrace.
Fly in the face of retribution
Make delight your bold solution
Let indulgence set you free
Save you from the working week
Release your mind from care and debt
Get hard and soft and warm and wet
Let sweaty spunky juices flow, let it happen
Be
Let go
Let go of all the ties that bind you
Rope you in contain confine you
Squeeze your vision, pare your needs
Stifle creativity
Plunder hope and splatter care
Steal your soul and leave it bare
Bound and gagged without consent
Leave you ravaged sullied spent
Tell tall tales, raise your game
Up the anti, take the blame
Wear it with pride
Display the damage that you hide
Let all disguises that you wear
Fall away and disappear
All your lust and all your magic
Tearing at the social fabric

All your power all your might
Seize the day
Reclaim the night
Own it, claim it, win it, name it
Take the hurts and let them heal you
Give play to all that you may feel to
Investigate it all, explore
There's something in you wanting more
Something in you needs to find
A liberty, an ease of mind
A sanctuary within your life
A breath, a gasp, a brief respite
To mollify, somewhat erase
The cruelty of this time this place
The angles of our living space.
Tits and ass and anarchy
Funky frocks and liberty
When indulged in fantasy
You alter your reality
When you allow yourself to play
At things that you may never say
At things that you were taught were wrong
Learn dirty rhymes and nasty songs
To sweetly sing yourself to sleep
Warm moist memories in your keep
When you do the things you like
It lifts your spirit, aids your life
When you allow yourself to go
Beyond the dark side then you'll know
That deep inside our souls does dwell

The key to that which makes us well
Carnal loves cure and expel
Our secrets and our shame as well

On my own head
I was well warned of the consequences
of letting go of my defences.
Told time and time and time again
the importance of one's own good name.
Instructed in the cold damnation
of a damaged reputation.
Informed that it was social death
to dance all night, take drugs, have sex,
Be seen out with dishevelled hair
and ladders in my stockings.
My skirt too short, my heels too high
and I should not be looking
Into passing cars that slow to let me by,
Or dawdling past the building sites
returning whistles with a smile.
I never, never, never should,
play with the gypsies in the wood
And say "No, no, I'll not abide"
when boys asked me to come outside.
Such conduct would be unbecoming,
my downfall quite deserved.
So I should keep away from men...
but no one mentioned girls.
I tried so hard to toe the line, I tried to guard my honour,
But I'm just a girl who can't say no, who can't resist an offer
Of a good time, the promise of a thrill.
I just say yes, I just love sex, I hope I always will,
And the wicked little slut I was has grown into a woman.
That wayward wanton jailbait child

whose parents shook their heads,
Stayed out all night just running wild,
who wouldn't cross her legs,
Has matured into a goddess who knows exactly,
What she needs.
Exactly how to get it.
I now do what I please.
My good intentions as they were,
were trampled and I was not deterred,
And all the lectures only served
to make me love those naughty girls,
Who smoked behind the bike sheds
and didn't make their beds,
Who drank cider at the boys' school
in their lunch breaks, and instead
Of doing homework, put on lipstick in their rooms,
Read dirty stories secretly... I hoped to be one soon.
Because I knew that the alternative
was not a way that I could live.
I knew I would enjoy life best
engaged in pleasures of the flesh.
So on my deathbed I'll remember
all the magic, all the splendour,
The many joyous escapades,
the lucky encounters I have made.
The one night stands, the flings, romances,
the mercy killings, the missing chances,
The random snogs, the beds, the bogs,
the alleys and the living rooms,
The underwear, the food we ate

and of course all of the tunes
That made the soundtrack to my my own erotic movies.
My pornographic lifestyle choice, comforts and amuses.
It's a work of art! Call me tart!
I'll wear the name with pride.
A slut like me should never be ashamed or have to hide
Behind convention. Be bound by social mores,
Because it's no one's fucking business
what goes on behind closed doors,
And no one's going to tell me what I can and can't explore.
No small minds will keep from me
the expanses of my liberty.
No petty rules will take control
of limiting my heart, my soul.
My sexual freedom is the cause
and, obviously, so is yours,
That sets off a chain reaction.
Repression is a rope that binds, a most unsightly fashion.
For underneath the norms that lie
are hidden agendas, quelled desires,
Fuel that feeds the fire of our oppression, our demise,
The owning of our senses
and the domination of our minds.
So I just might reclaim the night,
adorning it with fairy lights.
With mirrors, silks, and lots of toys,
bring dirty girls and nasty boys,
Hot, hot women, horny men,
anyone who wants to play and then
Wearing lipstick and red fuck-me shoes

we'll celebrate our lives and use
All our favourite party tricks
to get our rocks off get our kicks,
Get hot, get high, get off our heads
on the revolution in our beds.

Blinding
You can't show me a magazine
that recreates the things I see.
The stories that I take to bed, the filth I carry in my head.
There is no possibility, no words, no visibility,
Can approach the dreams that wander
Through my mind and into yonder fantasies,
A place where there is no disease.
No consent, no limitations, no uneasy situations.
No uncertainty, no cost, no hurts.
No one to judge me as perverse.
Somewhere at the heart of me
Lie things that no one ever sees,
Things that I would never share,
It's best that I should leave them there,
In the safe space of my mind
where boundaries need not be defined.
In my wild imaginings
I can shapeshift, I grow wings.
Engage with woman, man and beast alike.
Toy with human sacrifice.
I may strut or I may cower,
Rubber leather satin flowers,
Mouths and cocks and cunts and feet,
Tits and arseholes hands and teeth.
Debaucheries I dare to think
Depraved and wanton how I sink into base revelry,
Partake of all that pleases me,
And no I will not analyse
The origin of my desires.

I care not to read between the lines,
Nor question if these whims are mine.
Choose not to seek the references
Pertaining to my preferences.
For all that lives inside my thoughts,
Is lifted borrowed copied taught
To me at my mother's breast,
I drank it in with all the rest.
Learned my lessons oh so well,
What I should and should not tell.
Sick pictures seeded in my dreams.
The adverts, all the movie queens.
The TV and the Internet
Bombarding me with sex and death,
With dysmorphic permutations,
Unsavoury ejaculations
Pepper the fabric of my sex,
Imprinting me with well worn text.
Bedevilled by such magery
However could my mind be free?
Intoxicated with lush lies
How could my honour not decline?
The lowest commonest denominations.
The damnedest twisted permutations.
All of which occur to me,
Precipitate my beauty sleep,
With grunts and cries for lullabies,
Tingling flesh and trembling thighs.
Kisses, rope burns, stockings, blisters,
Rosie palm and her five sisters.

Cunt
Who are you calling cunt? Cunt!
Who dares call my name,
who summons the mother of all cunts?
And your mother too, y'cuntless wimp.
You think having a hole between your legs
makes you a woman?
Think again, you need balls to call yourself a cunt!
No cross-legged, dry-lipped virtuous virgins here!
I'm a right cunt I am,
a right fucking cunt,
wide open and ready
to eat you up for breakfast... and spit you out for lunch.
I've not been saving myself for prince charming,
you can stick your shining armour
cos I've noosed my own charger
and I rode it, bareback right into the fray,
Defending my own honour and my right to get fucked.
You'll not catch me hiding in a corner
deflowered and desolate,
a vapid vaginal victim of circumstances.
I'll fuck you right back you fucker,
because she's had 'em all this old cunt,
had 'em all and needed more.
You feast on the mouth of the universe
when you eat my pussy.
I permit your union with the goddess,
and should you worship there without due reverence
then your pathetic profanity petrifies your potence,
your loss is your own spirit

your scattered seed will spill in stale stains
and *our* holy communion with eternity
becomes mundane fuckery,
so fuck you if you think you can fuck me over.
This cunt's been fucked,
so many times she'll hardly even notice.
You'll need a few extra strings to your bow
if you're going to fuck this mother,
whet her lips,
cool her scorched earth,
lull her raging tides and discover,
if you may,
the lush shores of her sated appetite
where you can be still and whole and true for a while
before embarking, newly empowered.
No such sustenance to be had
from your cute perfumed fuck-me bitches
who'll lie back and take it
whimpering succubus babes
passive potency twisted into dangerous artifice
Plastic pleasantries surgically enhanced
till there's no cunt left at all!
Shaven and shorn with nothing there
but a neat clean slit for pissing or posing for porn.
No sculpted stitched up mockery of maidenhood
will move you
like my well oiled, pulsing, clenching love muscle.
My swollen, uncouth, squeezing, screaming, laughing cunt.
Perverts,
look at yourselves, call yourself a woman

with your baby doll bullshit and your girlie gloss?
What's it all about?
Where's your cunt, woman?
You've turned yourself into a parody of your daughter
and come to think of it,
How's *she* ever going to call herself a cunt
if she's all pink, pretty, princess paedophiles' delight
dressing up her forbidden fruit
like a fucking whore's boudoir?
Leave her alone,
you have no business there.
As if we didn't have enough to deal with,
here comes mutton dressed as lamb
with baby jailbait in tow.
Like a little baby beacon
welcoming all the wankers who are too limp
to face a cunt that bleeds unceremoniously,
fucks euphorically and births magnificently.
No,
better stick with your she-dolls,
sterile barren barbies,
marry your mincing mistresses
made up with malice aforethought.
Because you don't want me to show you a thing or two.
Lure you into a lush and heady courtship.
Lead you up the garden path, round the houses
and right up my street,
It won't be a blind alley.
Not unless you're running scared,
in which case,

you might just find yourself caught,
in a dead end
with a ball-busting bitch.
Doing your fucking head in
with my radical fucking feminism.
Ramming it down your throat again and again
until you choke on it
and call me a cunt.
Y' calling me a cunt?
I *am* C. U. N. T!
cunt
and your mother too.

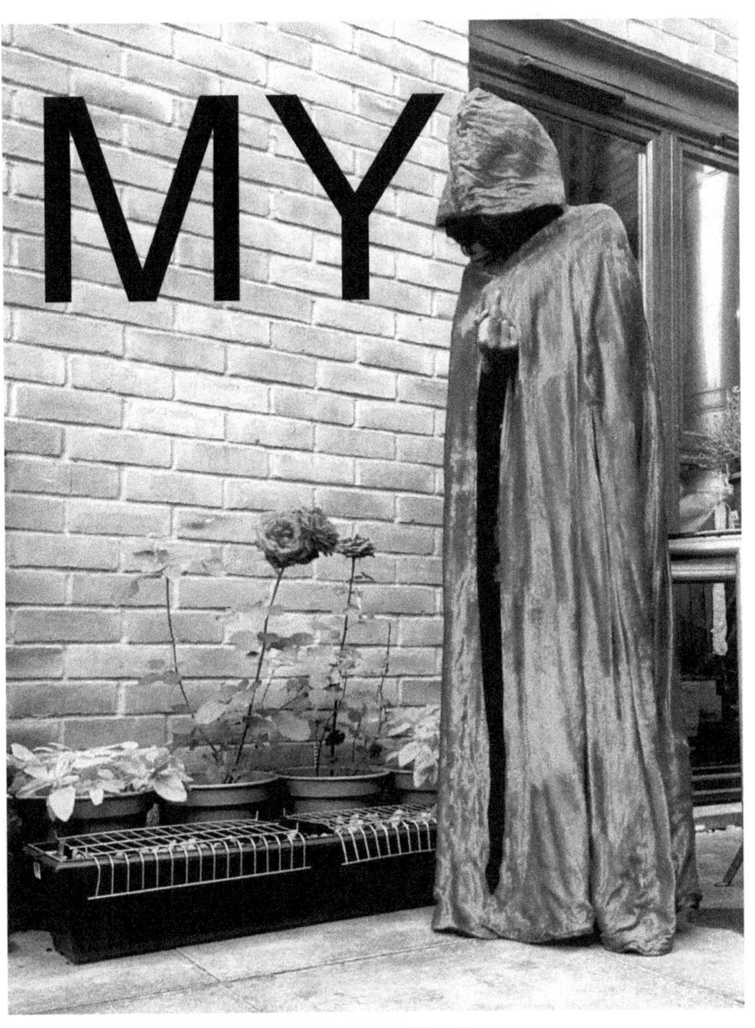

over MY dead body
La Nonika

Safe as houses
Que sera, sera, whatever will be will be.
It'll all come out in the wash.
Mind your manners.
Bide your time.
Don't look a gift horse in the mouth.
Stay in line.
Mind your step.
Be seen not heard.
I want doesn't get.
Don't ruffle your feathers.
Don't rock the boat,
Or get your knickers in a twist.
That's just the way the cookie crumbles.
That's just the way it is.
That's just the way of the world.
The bed is made, so lie in it.
Least said, soonest mended,
And don't look above the parapet.
What the eye doesn't see, the heart won't grieve.
Best leave well alone.
Keep your head down. Pass the buck.
Watch your mouth. Don't push your luck.
Don't dig too deep. Don't go too far.
Keep your counsel. Don't push too hard.
Take a look before you leap.
Take a rain check. Take it easy.
Take a chill pill. Wait and see.
Give it a break, Watch and wait.
Lock the door. Close the gate.

Stay inside. You can't hold back the tide.
You won't feel a thing.
Open wide.
Watch the world go by.
Watch time pass,
Paint dry.

Faithless
Faithless seeking nothing more
As businessman or media whore
Faithless
As consuming fool
Faithless
As a market tool as you consume and you destroy
The all-consuming pointless toys
That dull your mind and blunt your wit
That fill your head with pointless shit
That leaves no room for rumination
No time for the actualisation
Of the self and of the soul
And so you never will be whole
Never fit and never able
To read the code inside the fable
Seen it done it bought and sold
Dumbed down re-edited retold
Refurbished rehashed remarketed
So as to turn your pretty head
So as to tempt so as to tease
So as to excite
So as to ease
So as to keep so as to cosset
So as to keep you in that pocket
So as to lull and sooth and find you
So as to know and keep and bind you
So as to keep you never seeking
Questioning or disbelieving
So as to keep you

Blind you
Keep you
Faithless

Born to Shop
How much do you earn in your daily grind?
For what products do you yearn
To buy your peace of mind?
How much did you spend?
Where will it all end?
Will you get an ideal home?
A partner and the new iPhone?
Will you ever get the time?
Will you ever taste the wine
Made of the fruits of your hard labour?
Will you ever get to savour
The luxuries of the life of ease
You see in all the magazines?
Are you dreaming of a perfume
To make your life complete?
Or is there something else to buy
To make you the 'brand new me'?
Can you get it cheaper?
Can you get it off the cuff?
Designer-made identities – if you've got enough –
If you've got the wonga
then your black hair could be blonder,
And if you're clever, if you're sly
You will know what things to buy.
What to wear, what to eat, where to go, how to sleep
Who to talk to, what to say
What to think, how much to pay,
For an idea or a feeling or some comfort, or a fuck,
For a brand new way of living - or if you *really* are in luck,

Then your working life will all be spent
In pursuit of corporate dreams,
And as you scrimp and save and buy
You'll know what it really means,
To be living, be consuming.
Then one day when you die
You'll leave all of your possessions,
So you won't have lived a lie.
And when your children ask you
Who, where, why and when and what,
You can say "It's all right darling,"
And tell them "You were born to shop –
Born to shop, born to smoke
To eat baked beans and snort up coke"
The birthright of the lucky few,
The right to eat until we spew.
The freedom to choose your addiction.
Gambling, drinking or pulp fiction.
Stop here and buy one.
Did you know you needed it?
Get one for me Mum!
Feed them on a pile of shit.
Learn the brand names all by rote
And the jingles, every note,
Art of the times in advertising,
For a brain-dead public, is it surprising
The no-one remembers any more
What living life was like before
The advent of the multinational?
Oh, we have such privilege!

Just take a peek into my fridge
And see the labels gathered there
Feel the texture of my hair,
Courtesy of Silvikrin
Or touch my soft Max Factor skin.
Witness now my loss of weight,
There's Lean Cuisine upon my plate
But what of those without such luck?
A Telethon should raise a buck!
Raise my social consciousness
With slogans on a trendy vest.
Feed a migrant, plant a tree
Save a can – good old me!
I can be a caring consumer
But I need my car to get there sooner.
I feel I have the right to choose
Which washing powder should I use?
In the great free West the right to buy
And for the rest an open sky?
Acid rain falls from a hole.
Brand new deserts take their toll.
Esso, Big Mac, Unilever
Put trademarks on our souls forever,
But there is justice and we all share
The cancerous sun
And the poisonous air.

Working for The Mouse
Where were you going when you set out
on that journey from your parents' house?
What were you aiming to become
when your learning and your growing was done?
What did they tell you,
What did you see?
What did you make of opportunity?
What have you lost ?
What have you found ?
Were your mountains high?
Did your feet leave the ground?
Was your vision clear?
Was your goal in sight
Was the town bright red?
Was there thrill in the fight?
Did the means reach an end?
Did you find your way
To the vision that you saw that day?
Or did it get lost in the money go round?
The job that you got and the flat that you owned.
Did you stay late at the office,
Rush for the train,
Lie to the boss,
Eat Mcdonalds, again?
Did you wash it away with a movie or two?
Snuggle up with Disney
Just Mickey and you.
Did you wind up working for The Mouse?
Does he own your car, your house?

Does he own your soul as well ?
Is nine-to-five a living hell?
Does he own your hopes and dreams,
And your aspirations?
Does he book you by the hour
and take you on vacation?
Does he whisper in your ear,
Call you in and draw you near?
Soothing, sumptuous, pretty lies.
He's lying in your face.
Every ugly truth deny,
Make you out of place, out of time,
Out of sorts,
Out of your mind,
With longings for the fantasy.
Striving for it endlessly,
Perfect figure,
Perfect hair,
Perfect lives without despair,
Perfect smile,
Perfect teeth,
Perfect defects underneath.
Perfect depression,
Perfect obsession,
Perfect neurosis,
Perfect psychosis,
Perfect consumption,
Will be the redemption
And Barbie and Ken
will walk hand in hand.

The bright young hope of the master plan,
And no one is hungry
And no one is poor
If you open your heart and open your door
And everything they say is true!
See what The Mouse can do for you!

Without a paddle
Education sold my soul.
Packaged me and shipped me whole
into employment, life's enjoyment,
slowly slipping from my grasp.
Whilst kissing butt and ageing, fast.
With mortgages and loans and debts
hot on my heels at every step.
Now, looking back,
My youth departed,
Wishing I had never started,
To sell my time, exploit my talents
Overturn my work life balance.
The opulence I could achieve,
is getting harder to believe.
Homes and gardens, yachts and cars.
In my face, beyond my grasp.
Provide first-rate work for second-rate wages.
Scrimp and save for bloody ages.
Do without, don't lie in bed.
So our kids can get ahead.
Undervalued, underpaid,
Understandably enraged,
Under pressure, undermined,
Unrecognised, abused, maligned.
It all comes down to pounds and pence.
What you earned and what you spent.
What you saved, what you gave.
Who robbed you,
What you pissed away.

Pennies from heaven.
Bank notes from hell.
Futures in purgatory.
Will you rest well?
When investing in markets, buying options in darkness.
Trading in shares of a tragedy's plot,
As you harvest the flesh of the ones who have not.
Couture and technology, the wealth of our might.
The spoils of a lifestyle,
But no sign of a life.

Mine

I want the thing I want
I want it now, I need it now
I need the thing I want
The thing I need I want it now
I want to get it, need to get it
And I don't care how I get the thing I want
What it costs or where it's from
I need the thing I want
And my needs cannot be wrong
My needs are real
And I just feel
I want them satisfied
Don't want to be without things
Have my comfort compromised
I need the things I want
To feel all right and on the top
I need the thing I want
So I can add to what I've got.

Slices of life

Slices of life,
Laid out on a plate.
Handed to you while you vegetate.
And do you feel some empathy,
As you consume the agony?
Is it hard to swallow?
Do you choke?
On the bomb blast victims, or can you joke?
Can you make a meal of it?
Lighten the load with the spice of wit?
Right all the wrongs in heated debate,
Knowing you'd never hesitate,
To rise to the call, should the hour
Come when the masses realise their power.
But until then, you've got to get on.
It's not your fault it's all gone wrong,
And as you watch the news go by
You eat your dinner, as you sigh,
At the sight of severed limbs,
Howling women and other things.
That should give you nightmares,
But they don't,
It could get to you
But you won't
Let it bring you down or play on your mind.
'Cause you're 'media-wise' and your tastes are refined.
So little dead babies don't haunt your dreams
Not the eyes of the starving, nor watching blood stream,
Across pavements where corpses litter the streets

It won't bother you because, well, it's all meat.
To be packaged and processed for the media machine.
So you can devour fresh humans,
And your hands can stay clean.

To Market To Market
Screaming at me. Screaming all the time,
All the fucking time.
Ravaging the landscapes of my mind.
Oh my fragile mind!
Oh the barking of the hawkers invades my very sleep.
A cacophony of commerce to bring me to my knees.
Keep me wanting, keep me dreaming
of that for which I have no need
Indecent propositions, unclean and quite diseased.
A hysteria of images.
A lewd display of nothingness.
A cruel disgusting emphasis
Perverts all of that which I possess.
It's stalking me, assaulting me,
Cultural assault and battery.
Plagiaristic, voyeuristic,
debased, depraved, completely twisted.
Picking at me, poking at me,
mocking, grabbing, leering at me.
Whispering into my dreams
and in my waking constant streams
of dire and trite suggestions, bland and ugly things,
ill conceived convenience.
A trillion salesmen scream,
Screaming at me, screaming all the time.
All the fucking time.
Dismembering the pastures of our lives.
Oh our precious lives!
Reduced to mere consumption,

unthinking dumb compunction.
Need it want it get it have it.
Spent it lost it waste it trash it.
Design it market package sell it
All the way to hell and back it's
Screaming at them screaming at their minds
Oh, their flowering minds!
The sweet untainted gardens of their lives
Oh our children's lives,
Are desecrated annihilated
Crapped on, conned and then castrated.
A global search for what is not
Of consequence, intrinsic rot.
Is decaying in the corner. Its stench permanent and vile.
Its moulding spores now spreading,
Its evil always treading
Heavy on the psyche,
Crushing to the heart.
Controlling deluded sensibilities,
Suggesting sick activities.
Poison pens, tragic tunes, puerile pictures
Vast extremes so big, so bright.
Flashing, strobing 3D shite
Is everywhere and all the time.
Is deafening, it mutes, it blinds.
Is screaming at me, screaming at me.
Screaming.

To Those Of Us Who Would Bear Arms

To those of us who would bear arms,
who would bear malice.
Hold to ransom, bring to harm,
Dominate, subordinate.
For power, cash or simple hate.
Your reputation does precede you,
The epic tales of all the greed you
Stole and stored.
All the human beings you whored.
All the lives that you have sold.
The lies the Children have been told.
The great technicians of the ages
Have splattered the bile across history's pages.
With wood and with iron and atoms and will.
Crafting destruction with infinite skill.
Sure of the accurate aim of the mission.
To kill, to dismember to slaughter to render
The inhumane cries of the tortured, remember,
How bloodletting curdles the future, and lies,
Make cosy excuses that cover our eyes.
From the depths of depravity deep in the harm
By those of us who would bear arms.
To those of us who would claim the lands,
would claim the oceans
Close them keep them, name them, treat them
With callous scorn and disrespect.
Leave them poisoned, foul and wrecked.
Beyond the reach of those who care,
For the warmth in the sun and the breath in the air.

The property you're passing on
Harbours the truth of all the wrongs you never righted
Those you displaced, the lives you blighted.
The conquerors of history's pages
Have laid the bonds across the ages.
With mandates, covenants and deeds.
Spread ownership like infectious disease.
In cut crystal glass houses, built on guilt
And other people's sweat, other people's labour,
Other people's time, how you sip and how you savour
Your ill-gotten gains
Your malodorous profits
Your trust funds and shares
Your profits, our losses.
The miscreants you breed
The earth that you damned
When you hounded the people from the land.

Pester Power
Give us your children,
The ones we don't fuck, we'll eat.
Put them through the mill and churn them out as meat.
Creep into their hearts, into their minds,
Steal them away, leave none behind.
Give us your children,
The ones we don't kill, we'll maim.
They'll follow the piper, right under the train.
Innocent victims shivering and sore,
Lashing, and caning, and rubbing them raw.
Give us your children
The ones we don't lose, we'll waste.
We'll savour the flavour of chicken flesh as we taste,
And ready the infants to consume the lie.
Young lives fresh and fattened
And baked in a pie.
Give us your children
The ones who can see, we'll blind,
Give us your children
The ones who can run, we'll find.
We will make them fear the truth,
Power the machine with the blood of youth,
Twist their bodies, fuck their heads,
Sell their souls, leave them dead,
Devour their corpses, rob their graves,
They're cannon fodder,
Market slaves.

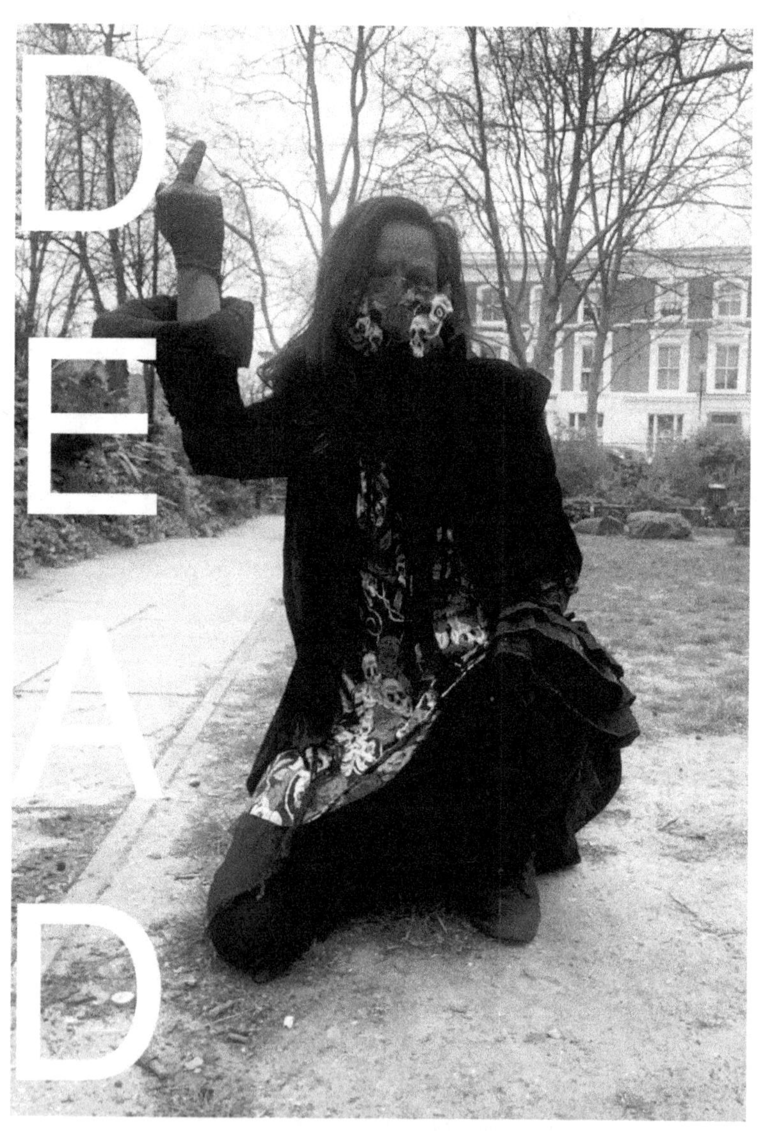

over my DEAD body
La Nonika

Shut the fuck up
Shut the fuck up.
Fuck off and die.
I'll dance on your grave when you've choked on that lie.
When you're swallowing shit, you'll regurgitate it.
When you've wasted your space, there'll be nothing to miss.
Shut the fuck up.
You poison the air.
Go smother yourself in pathetic despair.
No point, and no passion,
Your fear and your loathing,
A habit, a fashion,
Wrapped round you, exposing
Idiot nihilism,
Fatuous cynicism,
Cruel and heartless apathy.
The antithesis of liberty.
Shut the fuck up.
Shut your fucking face.
Your ideas blight the human race.
If you don't care, then we don't need you.
It's not worth what it costs to treat you.
Cure your sallow sickly thoughts.
Disseminate the crap you've bought.
In soundbites, your putdowns, your comebacks, your jibes,
Make soul-crushing pastimes, belittle our lives.
You've seen it, you've heard it, you've done it before,
Genned up on it, in the know.
You know the score.
Snigger at me with my heart on my sleeve.

With your clever arse self, you're a social disease.
Shut the fuck up, shut up, shut up please,
Contain your gross verbosities.
The concepts that you disregard.
The subtleties you miss.
The thesis is beyond your grasp,
So you just take the piss.
So genocides make anecdotes,
And tragedies give rise,
To jumped-up, dumbed-down wisecracks,
That end all conversation.
Fill the void with knock-backs,
Prevent the instigation,
Of anything challenging, anything new,
Anything noble, all because you,
Exist alone in self-disgust.
Your disdain for humanity shows me as much.
And I hope that you know, and I know that you care,
In the still of the night when there's nobody there.
Then it matters, so much you can hardly bear it
It matters so much that you spend all day,
Matters so much that your only defence is
Trying to keep the demons at bay.
The wrongs you're not blind to, the truths you deny.
The filth in your mind, and the shit in your eyes.
Your moronic throwaway rhetoric.
Your barbarous commentary makes me sick.
Because you are to blame, and you are the cause.
And the burden of shame and the fault,
It's all yours.

Really? Is this how it is?
What the actual fucking fuck
Is going fucking on?
How can we have messed it up so badly?
We've got it all so tragically wrong!
Life, it isn't hard to understand,
In fact, it's mostly easy to conceive.
It's the staggering incompetence
That actually beggars belief.
The idiocy so commonplace
In, apparently, the entire human race,
Provides for constant consternation
At the level of debate,
The ignorant procrastination
Of addressing the sorry state
We seem to have got ourselves in,
There is no one else to pin it on
And we're not doing anything,
And when we do, it's not for long.
We haven't solved any problems,
We made them, and then made them much much worse,
With our spasticated ideas
We make sure everyone gets hurt,
In one way or another,
Take your pick,
Any way you like.
You can have starvation or displacement,
Or you could try a war crime for size
Have any one you fancy!
Or if they don't float your boat,

You could go for sexist racist classist child abuse
And see which one you like the most.
Maybe eco death will interest you?
We do a great line in that!
Both animal and vegetable,
We probably make minerals feel like crap
What a bunch of stupid stinky cunts
We are to have allowed,
Such a cock-up to progress unchecked
Its tumescence standing proud.
Global in its proportions.
Universal in its scope.
Minuscule in solutions.
Our world heritage is a joke.
Look at us! Shifting deck chairs
On the Titanic while it sinks
Debating our identities
And trying work out what we think.
In case nobody's noticed
There's an ice age on its way!
It really doesn't matter much
Who may or may not be to blame.
Because unless we fix up sharpish
We are going to die out, horribly.
With lots of pain and anguish.
But then we're good at that, aren't we?
We are excellent at wreaking havoc
We're most proficient at causing shite
We utterly rock when it comes to
Denying liberty and life,

To all and goddamn sundry,
We won't stop at sentient beings.
Oh no, that's not enough for us!
We have to poison everything
We can get our mucky hands on.
Drunk on stupidity we bring
The entire good earth to its crumbling knees.
The air and the sky and the sun and the trees.
Unnoticed except in photographs.
Unheeded as all that will last.
When we have wiped our asshole selves out
When the Gaia sighs her relief.
From the viewpoint of eternity,
This sorry sojourn seems quite brief.
Oh please, can we go home now?
Can we just call it done?
Can we read a different story?
Because I don't like this one.
The heroes are all toss pots.
The princess is a bitch.
The dragon's had its balls cut off,
And some idiot burned the witch.
There's gonna be tears before bedtime.
Wracking, heaving sobs all night long.
Raging, weak, terrified victims,
Of so many unspeakable wrongs.

Yearn, At A Loss?

Where is it? Where is it? Where is that which is lost?
Where is that which should dwell at the centre of us?
Where is it? Where is it? How could it be gone?
How is it the hearth is lost from the home?
How that the women know not to make bread ?
Have forgotten the words that their grandmothers said?
How have the men lost the kindling of flame?
The ways of the wilds, their forefathers' names?
Where will we find for us such as we need ?
To pass to our children a solid belief,
In moonlight and magic in love and in joy,
impart to them skills that their lives can employ
In the mending and making that needs must be done,
How goes the salvage, the righting of wrongs?
Where is it? What is this? How could this be?
The caging of skies and the slaughter of trees!
What is it? What is it? What madness is this?
What malady rages? What sickness persists?
Where are the mindful? Where are the sages?
What of the temples, the wisdom of ages?
Where are all the open spaces?
What of all the sacred places?
What of flowers?
What of seeds?
Of virgin lands?
Of open seas?
Where have all the forests gone?
And what about the summer sun?
No longer kind but burns my skin

And food that poisons! Everything
Seems lost and broken
What is there now to have hope in?
What is there now to believe?
What now left that still runs free?
What is truth and what is lies
Must be known to recognise
That which endures and is divine,
From that which is a waste of time.
Who has the blueprint? Who rights the signs?
Who makes the healing? Who knows of the time
For living and dying, for futures and pasts?
Will the dust of our journey bring us home at last?
Where are all the safety nets?
The guarantees, the safer bets?
Where are all the easy routes, the short cuts
Where are all the loops?
To guide us through the city's maze
To lead us to those halcyon days
Where we will never want again
Nor feel the cold
Nor see the pain
Who is it nurtures the talents required?
Who gains the knowledge for us to reach higher?
Our people are scattered
Our customs forgotten
The fruit of our loins
Grow up twisted and rotten
Our homes have been raided
Our blood has been spilled

What is it? What is it?
That will comfort these ills?
Where is the remedy for the blight of the ages?
What of the bards and the seers and the mages?
Who are the heroes?
What chance have we got
To seek out and to savour that which is lost?

Yearn, Hometime
What are our ways
And where are our means
For the making of health
And the reading of dreams?
How lies our life
And what is our worth
In the measure of time
We walk on the earth?
Who distils tinctures?
Who cures the herbs?
Who has the cunning?
Who knows the words?
Who sings the dream time?
Where are the guides?
Who'll teach the children
The ways of the tribe?
Who speaks with the beasts?
Who charts the skies?
Who keeps the stories
Awake and alive?
Where are the seasons
That keep us in step?
Who is it knows
Where our heirlooms are kept?
Where are the Old Ways
The tales of the wives?
Who makes the matches?
How will we survive
If the customs and teachings

Are fallacies, pride?
Are the touches of magic
Now lost from our hands?
Are the herds struck dumb
All hope lost to the lands?
Are our people all weeping
In fear and in loss?
If we can't find our way
At what price, at what cost
Will we fumble in darkness
Mistaken and sad
In the tragic belief
That the best has been had?
For infernal ages
Grow ugly and bland
Seek out comfort, get cosy
Get stuck, fall asleep
Squander the gifts
That we have in our keep?
Will the ways of the world
Become hungry and vile
Will our spirit be taken
With profit and style?
Does the work of our lives
Gentle our world?
Are the words that we speak
Of a kind to be heard?
Is there love in the justice?
Are there winners in wars?
Is there guilt in our knowing?

Will anyone pause?
To take in the meanings?
Take time to take stock
Of the gains we could make
seeking that which is lost?
Our history's seeds
Have been spent in rough sowing
Our sense has been scattered
Through labelling and owning
Can our re-education be honest and kind?
Can terror and loathing be left, be confined?
As we seek our humanity,
Follow the course.
Will the light in the tunnel
Return to the source?

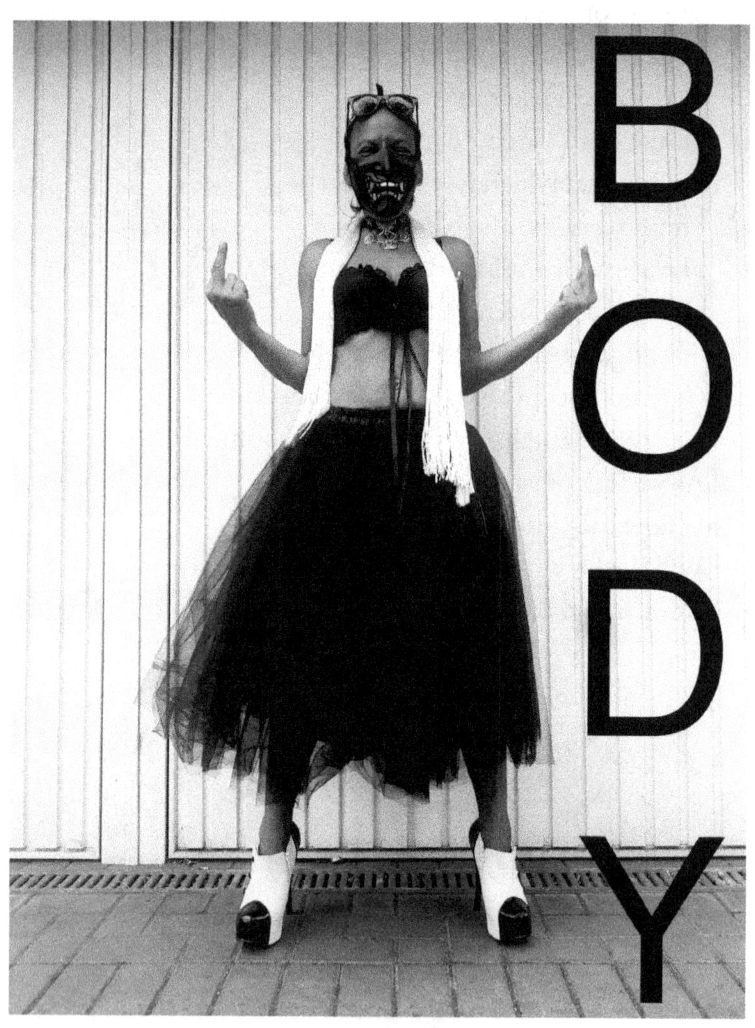

N.O.C
Poetry resides not in the annals of history
or the corridors of power
Sold into comfort by an annual stipend.
Instead it has its birth
In the uncouth gutters
Wherein resides the pain in the soul of humanity.
Through the horror of war
And the agonies of deprivation
The need for poetry arises.
And as the rising sound of the dispossessed
Bleeds into the deafening dominance
Of a dumbed-down comfort culture
That seeks only to replicate
its own narcissistic vision of itself
So rises the shrill and callous howling of the powerful.
See them baying like hounds
For deference and humiliation
As they set upon the bards and the seers.
To create in the midst of destruction
To find art in the midst of hate
To speak out unabashed in the face of rage and ridicule
Such is the path of the poet.
Those who speak of truth
Walk tall in the knowledge
That it is indeed an honour
To be so insulted.
Backstreet dealers
Fences, whores,
Gypsies, rent boys, thieves and all

Slackers, squatters, scammers, wasters,
Fingersmiths and entertainers,
Problem children, mental cases
And addicts occupy dark places
The alleys in between the status.
Not a shred of class between them
Just a love of life and freedom.
Unkempt and uneducated.
Untrained, uninitiated.
Unaspiring, unclean.
Uncouth, untalented,
Unseen,
Unheard-of, uncared-for, underrated,
Misunderstood, misrepresented.
On the fringes, on the edge
On the streets, off the ledge
Raise your voices one and all
Stand united, else we'll fall
Raise your voices one and all
Stand united, else we'll fall.

I'll hum it, You play it
You be the paddy,
I'll be the nigger,
One of us borrow a dog.
We can play the race card first,
See if we get the nod.
Then you can claim working class disenfranchisement,
I'll vindicate women's rights.
If we both bring up gender bent,
We can keep the show running all night.
Then let's go on to mental health,
Blatant sexism and the absence of wealth.
Throw in a bit of loss of the land,
That should give us the upper hand.
Then when they have got that bit,
You tell them about the disadvantages,
In education and in health care,
Then I'll come in with inadequate welfare.
A bit of insecurity might go down well,
We both have a housing story to tell.
If we pitch it well and spin it right,
Someone that can do something actually might,
Wake the fuck up,
Get with the programme.
Or we might get kicked out
For disrupting the meeting.

The hand that rocks the cradle
The hand that rocks the cradle,
Should also rock the boat.
Do the shopping,
Fight oppression,
Do the laundry,
Stay afloat.
Bear the children,
Hold a job down, and utilise her vote.
Love the children, bring them up, well.
And write the school a note.
And while she's at it there's the homeless, and the hungry,
and the sick.
And the lonely, and the aged
Oh yeah, and the housework, quick!
And she'd like to fit a bath in,
And find time to paint her nails.
With all of that and more to do
She isn't going to fail,
To rise to the occasion,
With the necessary flair,
With her head high and her eyes bright,
In her favourite party wear.
She'll be willing.
She'll be winning.
She'll be walking out, in style
Ringing changes in the future,
Making pies up in the sky.
Stand up sister, bring the baby
Reach out

Don't pass the buck,
Because tomorrow's in the balance,
And we're running out of luck.
The hand that rocks the cradle,
Wields the power - yeah, that's you!
And what we need around this planet
Is a shift in our attitudes.
To the women who give us so much of themselves
Who pick up our shit, and then store it as well!
Who remember the birthdays.
Who clean up the crap.
Who don't get paid
And don't get thanked.
No status, no pension, no sick pay, no wage
No prospects, promotion and no holidays.
No lunch break,
No union
No company car
So keep on rocking that boat,
Till they know who we are.

Kitchen songs
My sisters' arms are warm and strong
Their voices rich with kitchen songs
And in their eyes are joys and sorrows
Broken dreams and bright tomorrows
Troubles many, praises few
Endless lists of things to do
Births and deaths and lives go on
The composition of their songs
Which ripple out into the future
empowered in the state of nurture.
My sisters' arms are warm and strong
Their voices rich with kitchen songs
And in the creases of their faces
Are memories of the human races
Loving made and children born
Broken nights and early dawns
The cornerstones of education
The alchemy of our creation
Mapping out, as they are able
The secrets of the kitchen table

Out of the Dolls House
They came out of the dolls house crying
"Why be a wife?"
They came out of the kitchens saying
"There must be more to life!"
They counted up statistics
Burned their bras
Wiped off their lipsticks
Some found G-spots, some took courses
Others ceased to shave their legs
Still others went for therapy to straighten out their heads
Yes, there was discussion and debating
Reclamation reinstating
Self-discovery, recovery
As they forged along the path
Learning how to be assertive in their masturbation class.
Now there's women in the cabinet,
and there's women in the church
In the medical profession and the law - for what it's worth
Herstory has come out in print
Both hard and paperback
And when they make the movie,
well that's going to be a crack -
Because some of us are waiting
For our power shoulder pads
To make us liberated
Like the women in the ads
Some of us are waiting for someone to do something
For the poor girls, and the fat girls
And the junkies, and the whores

And the mums in bed and breakfasts
And the well - need I say more?
It seems our sisters in the movement
Have left behind their roots
Gone off to have careers
They've given Shaz and Trace the boot
Because they still wear white stilettos
And they have too many kids
They like to watch 'Eastenders'
And that's the way it is.
Because some of us are cleaners
And some of us are wives
Some of us work in Tesco's
Many women spend their lives
Making ends meet
Making sure the kids eat
Putting shoes on their feet
Just keeping order
Just taking care
Because it needs to be done
Because nobody's there
To take any notice or light up the sky
Because it's not an achievement to simply get by
So those of us on the front line just slip through the net
We haven't got wages for housework just yet
You can with a Nissan, but can you without?
Textbook feminism never did have the clout
It takes more than orgasm
And more than a vote
And more than a salary - so sisters, take note:

There may have been changes but it ain't no great shakes
While there's still battered women, anorexics, date rapes
There's girls in Doc Martens out drinking in pubs
And cocktail dresses out dancing in clubs
But there's millions more in the shops and estates
In the launderettes, the play parks, outside the school gates
Invisible women, they really are there
If we listen to *them* then we might get somewhere.

In Our Time
Here at this crucial hour
Exists an infinite space between the moments
Between the end of the past
and the beginning of the future
Between yesterday and tomorrow
Here we can make the choice to assess the tumbling events
That have catapulted us through our lives
moment by moment
How did you spend the time just gone?
Did you treasure those minutes one by one?
Did you lend your strength to Mother Earth?
Is the cost of your keep a measure of your worth?
Do you speak out or rest in silence
Supporting the terror and the violence?
Did you make do and mend
or did you cop out and spend ?
Your ill-gotten gains on the global slave market?
It could be here, could be seconds away
From this moment on, a brand new way
A brand new chance, a brand new choice
To free your mind and raise your voice
Against the sinister machinations of the Powers-That-Be
In a cold world where only the markets run free
Against the sustained attack on all things true
Where the pavements are hard, and the buildings are cruel
Against the propagation of the war
That bolsters the rich
And beggars the poor
And when the worst has come, and all are fallen

When the madness reigns and all is bedlam
When cruelty ravages and all live in fear
At this, the darkest hour of the night
And of the ages
Peace is in the hands of the few
Those of us who can eat and sleep in safety
Rest in the crucible of opportunity
In the space between time, we can alter our lives
And turn our privileges into power
Wield our liberty for justice
In this eternity between events
This brief respite in the moment of time
Offers a place to stop.
To gather our minds and our energies
To ready the force of our will
And unleash a torrent of joy
In a brilliant new direction
For the hope of all humanity
For a future worth living for
A truth worth dying for
An earth worth crying for
And a quality of life that is so much more than a living
It's time to start again
Are we ready?
Then let's go -
The time is ripe
It's time to show
The world we really care
That we will
And that we dare

It's time to start again
Create a new world, create a new life
We can change the world we can make it come right
Make this the time your revolution
Turn the heads of institutions
Make this the day we change our ways
Summon all our might to say
Enough is enough, stop the madness
Enough is enough, the future is now
Enough is enough, stop the madness
Enough is enough, the future is now
Dare to proclaim it, to say it, to name it
Peace in our time, peace in our time
Dare to believe it, to want it, to dream it
Peace in our time, peace in our time
Dare to work for it, to never ignore it
Peace in our time, peace in our time
Dare to defend it, to build and extend it
Peace in our time, peace in our time
Because we are the hope of humankind
Because the future is now, create peace in our time
Because here is the place, and we draw the line
Because the future is now, create peace in our time
Because the earth is home to yours and to mine
Because the future is now, create peace in our time
The power of the individual is a force for change
That lies within you
Your life is the vehicle
through which you express the intention of your spirit
Grow a little each day

And thereby ease the darkness
One lumen at a time
Rise to the challenge of the age
with honour and with courage
And we will bring light to the world
With the glory of our greater selves.

Restart
The global war is hotting up
The ecosystem's out of luck
Society is cracking up
And there are no answers to the questions that I'm asking
We've wasted all the energy
We're running out of history
And the solutions to the problems that I'm posing
Are categorically being ignored
Our swift demise is being assured
I'm nervous, tetchy, I'm appalled
I'm powerless, we're fucked -
I'm going out dancing
I'm going to lose myself in play
Let chemicals wash it away
I'm not going to rant
I'm going to rave
I'm going out dancing -
If powdered joy is all I've left
Without elation I am bereft
No reason we should sit and wait
For sanction - may we celebrate?
We'll raise our glasses, take a sip
Toasting the apocalypse -
If we're burning, then I'm going to fly
If we're drowning, well, I'm getting high
If the world ends in war
We might as well party
We'll vote for ourselves
Get high and mighty

Build towers of Babel
Watch them fall
Down will come baby,
Cradle and all.
And as Babylon crumbles and the dust comes near
We'll smell the hate
And feel the fear
Creeping in on all that we hold dear
And when the flames come close, we'll fucking cheer!
Because our bitter twisted hearts are broken
Ripped asunder, left wide open
The tears that well up in my eyes
Vain protest, pointless alibis
That scarcely banish my reaction
My complacency and my inaction
Atrocities I've sat and watched
Genocide, and other such
Ordinary, everyday
Crimes that fill our lives each day
I'm not brave, I'm not strong
The best I can manage is a protest song
I'm not wise and I'm not clever
And I won't risk my life - not ever
I won't leave my European home
To fight for peace in the danger zone
I can't fight back 'cause I've been whipped
I can't feed the hungry or nurse the sick
Aggressive marketing masks my voice
I'm branded into a lifestyle choice
Stitched up by a Nike flash

Frittering my hard-earned cash
On escape routes for the heart and mind
I'm seeking out alternative kinds
Of company whispering undertones
Luring me away from home
Where under beats an inside music
I can dull that pain and lose it
Safe in rhythm, lost in a mix
More a bandage than a fix
Knowledge weak and conscience yearning
I can but fiddle while Rome is burning
Let it burn, let it bleed,
Let it ache, let it freeze
Let it sigh, let it simper
Will we snivel as we whimper?
It wasn't me, it wasn't mine -
It's not my fault, it isn't fair -
I didn't do it, I didn't see -
It's not my fault I wasn't there -
It isn't right or true or just
There's no denying, if feel we must
Luxuriate in privilege
Savour every second
A taste of every pleasure take
Turn these into our weapons
With wild hair and sweating limbs
We'll sing another kind of hymn
We'll raise our voices, elevate ourselves
Above the mass of hate
Above the bullshit, above the lies

Pride will fall but passion flies
High above and on forever
Watch and learn and never, ever
Lose your vision of the distance
Never guilty of assistance
Of working for the national debt
Or saving up for when it's wet
Throw all caution
Lose all care
The end is coming
Everywhere
The beginning is about to start
An idea nestling in your heart
Waiting for you, waiting for me
To dance that dream into reality.

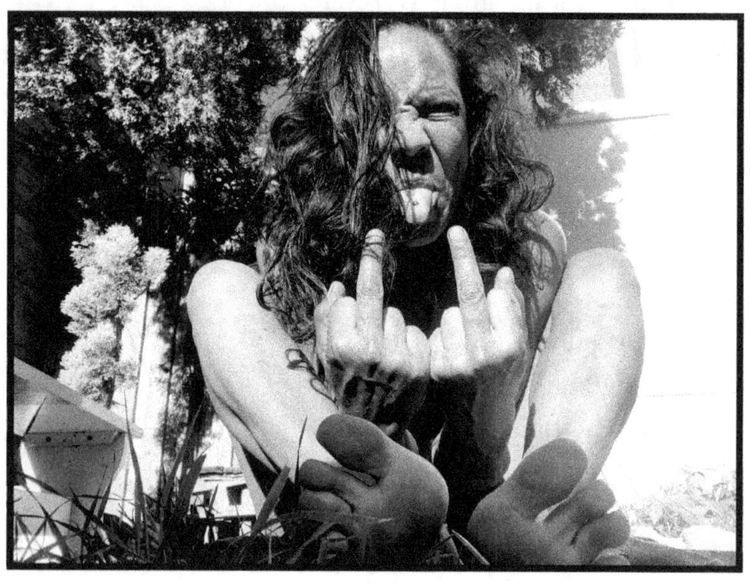

Centerfold
La Nonika